Bob Chilcott

Carols 2

*10 carol arrangements
for mixed voices*

MUSIC DEPARTMENT

OXFORD
UNIVERSITY PRESS

OXFORD
UNIVERSITY PRESS

Great Clarendon Street, Oxford OX2 6DP, England
198 Madison Avenue, New York, NY 10016, USA

Oxford University Press is a department of the University of Oxford.
It furthers the University's aim of excellence in research, scholarship,
and education by publishing worldwide

Oxford is a registered trade mark of Oxford University Press
in the UK and in certain other countries

11

ISBN 978-0-19-336507-0

Music origination by Jeanne Roberts
Printed in Great Britain on acid-free paper by
Halstan & Co. Ltd, Amersham, Bucks

Contents

Composer's note

I wrote this set of arrangements towards the end of 2005, and decided to dedicate them to some of the choirs and individuals with whom I have a close association. Three of the pieces are reworkings of arrangements I had written before: 'Il est né' was originally written in 1983 for the vocal group The Light Blues, and 'Away in a manger' was written in 1992 for the King's Singers and the Toronto Symphony Orchestra—in this one the audience always joined in! 'Sussex Carol' was originally written for upper voices for the volume *World Carols for Choirs*. The others are completely new, and the accompanied carols can be performed either with piano, or organ if appropriate, or in their orchestrated versions.

I am very grateful to Jane Griffiths for all her work on this volume.

Orchestral parts for the accompanied carols are available to hire from the publisher.

for Jonathan Rathbone and the Barnet Choral Society

Away in a manger

Anon., 19th cent.

Melody: W. J. Kirkpatrick (1838–1921)
arr. BOB CHILCOTT (b. 1955)

*Alternatively, bars 4–22 can be sung by *tutti* sopranos or *tutti* altos.
Orchestral material is available to hire from the publisher: hp, str

lit - tle Lord Je - sus a - sleep on the hay.

p

S.
A.

T.
B.

(TUTTI)
mp

The cat - tle are low - ing, the

mp

*The cat - tle are— low - ing, the— ba - by a -

mp

ba - by a - wakes, But— lit - tle Lord Je - sus no cry - ing he

- wakes, But— lit - tle Lord Je - sus no— cry - ing he makes. I

*If desired, the audience/congregation may join in with singing the melody from bar 24 until the end.

by me for ev-er, and_ love me, I pray. Bless all the dear chil-dren in_

thy ten-der care, And_ fit us for hea-ven, to_ live with thee

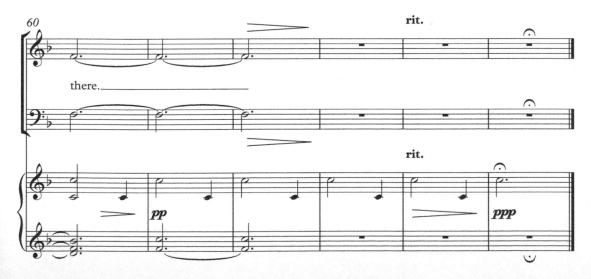

there._

for Simon Halsey and the CBSO Chorus

Coventry Carol

From the Pageant of the
Shearmen and Tailors (15th cent.)

English trad.
arr. BOB CHILCOTT

Orchestral material is available to hire from the publisher: fl, ob, 2cl, bsn, 2hn, str

might, In his own sight, All young chil -

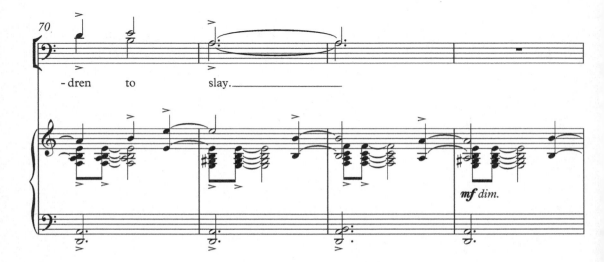

- dren to slay.

Lul - ly, lul - la, thou lit - tle ti - ny

child, By by, lul - ly, lul - lay, thou lit - tle ti - ny child,___

By by, lul - ly, lul - lay.___

That woe is me, Poor child for thee! And ev - er

morn and day, For thy part - ing Nei-ther say nor sing

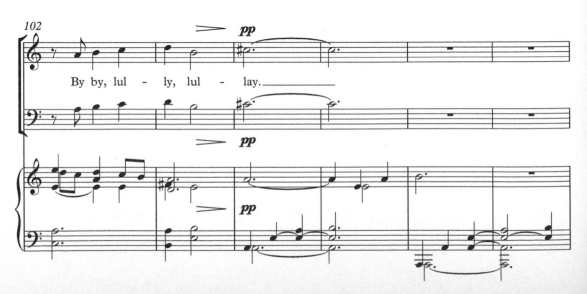

By by, lul - ly, lul - lay.

Lul-ly, lul-la, thou lit-tle ti-ny child, By by, lul-ly, lul-lay, thou lit-tle ti-ny child,___ By by, lul-ly, lul-lay.___

for Steve Jones and the City Chamber Choir

Gaudete!

Piae Cantiones, 1582

arr. BOB CHILCOTT

Orchestral material is available to hire from the publisher: fl, ob, 2cl, 2bsn, 2hn, 2tpt, timp, str

Chri - stus   est   na – tus   Ex   Ma – ri – a

Vir – gi - ne:__ gau - de – te!   E - ze - chie - lis   por – ta

Clau-sa per-tran-si – tur; Un-de Lux est or – ta,___ Sa-lus in-ve-ni – tur.

Gau - de - te!___ gau - de - te!___

Gau - de - te! gau-de-te! Chri-stus est na - tus Ex Ma - ri - a

Gau - de - te!___ gau - de - te!___

Gau - de - te! gau-de-te! Chri-stus est na - tus Ex Ma - ri - a

p sempre

Vir - gi - ne:___ gau-de - te!   Er - go nos-tra con-ci - o

Psal-lat iam in lus - tro;   Be-ne-di-cat Do-mi-no: Sa-lus Re-gi nos - tro.

Gau - de - te! gau - de - te! Chri - stus est na - tus

Ex Ma - ri - a Vir - gi - ne:___ gau - de - te!

Gau – de – te! gau – de – te! Chri – stus est na – tus

Ex Ma – ri – a Vir – gi – ne:__ gau – de – te!

for Mark Sirett and the Cantabile Choirs, Kingston, Ontario

Il est né, le divin enfant

French trad.
arr. and trans. BOB CHILCOTT

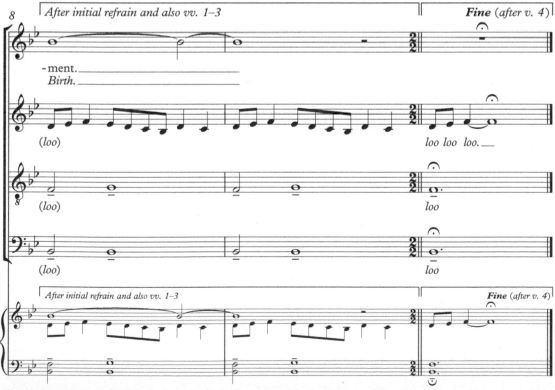

VERSE 3

for David Wordsworth and the Addison Singers

Jesus, Jesus, rest your head

American trad.
arr. BOB CHILCOTT

Orchestral material is available to hire from the publisher: hp, str

Have you heard a-
Have you heard a-bout our Je-sus,

-bout our Je - sus, How the shep-herds went to the sta - ble
Have you heard a - bout his fate? How the shep - herds

for the Amabile Choirs, London, Ontario

Jingle, Bells

Words and melody: J. Pierpont (1822–93)
arr. BOB CHILCOTT

Orchestral material is available to hire from the publisher: 2fl, 2ob, 2cl, 2bsn, 2hn, sleigh bells, glock, hp, str

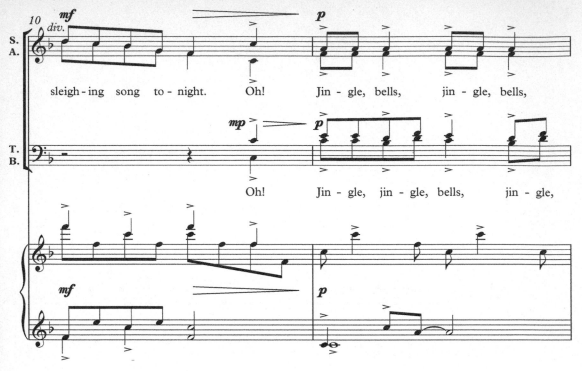

one - horse o - pen sleigh! Oh! Jin - gle, bells, jin - gle, bells,

one - horse o - pen sleigh! Oh! Jin - gle, jin - gle, bells, jin - gle,

jin - gle all the way; Oh, what fun it is to ride in a one-horse o - pen

bells, jin - gle, jin - gle all the way; what fun it is to ride in a one-horse o - pen

for the BBC Singers

Still, still, still

German trad.
arr. and trans. BOB CHILCOTT

for David Lawrence and the City of Birmingham Young Voices

Sussex Carol

English trad.
arr. BOB CHILCOTT

Orchestral material is available to hire from the publisher: 2fl, 2ob, 2cl, 2bsn, 2hn, 2perc (triangle, glock), str

News of great joy, news of great mirth, News of

our mer - ci - ful King's birth.

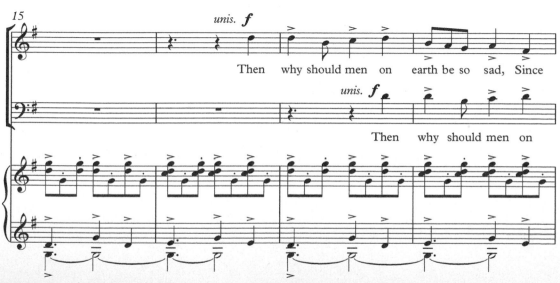

Then why should men on earth be so sad, Since

Then why should men on

When from our sin he set us free,_____ All for

to gain our li - ber - ty?_____

SOPRANO *f*

When sin de - parts be -

When

for Sheila Harrod and the Kentwood Showchoir

We wish you a merry Christmas

Trad. West Country carol
arr. BOB CHILCOTT

Orchestral material is available to hire from the publisher: fl, cl, 2hn, 2tbn, 2perc (drum kit, bongos), str

you and your kin; We wish you a mer-ry Christ-mas And a

hap - py New Year.

Now bring us fig - gy
Now bring us some fig-gy pud - ding, Now bring us some fig-gy

pud - ding, And bring some, bring some out

pud - ding, Now bring us some fig-gy pud - ding, And bring some out

DESCANT

Good tid - ings we bring To__ you and your kin; We

S.
A.

here. Good tid - ings we bring To__ you and your kin; We

T.
B.

here.

wish you a mer-ry Christ-mas And a hap-py_____ New

Year._____

And we

won't go un-til we've got some, We won't go un-til we've got some, And we

won't go,___ won't go,___ won't go,___ won't go,___

for the Taipei Chamber Singers

What child is this?

English trad.
arr. BOB CHILCOTT

William Chatterton Dix (1837–98)

Christ the King,___ Whom shep - herds guard___ and ang - els sing:

Haste, haste___ to___ bring him praise,___ The Babe,___ the Son___ of

Ma - ry.___

mp

Why lies___ he here_____ in such

unis.
mp

Why lies he in___ such mean es - tate___ Where

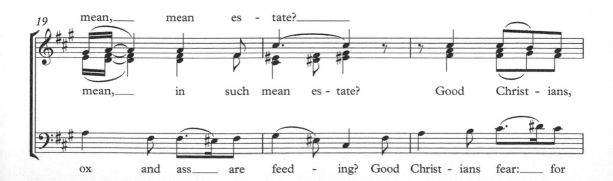

mean,___ mean es - tate?_____

mean,___ in such mean es - tate? Good Christ - ians,

ox and ass___ are feed - ing? Good Christ - ians fear:___ for

fear:_____ The Word___ is___ plead - ing.

sin - ners here___ The si - lent Word__ is plead - ing.

Nails, spear___ shall_ pierce him through, The cross be borne__ for

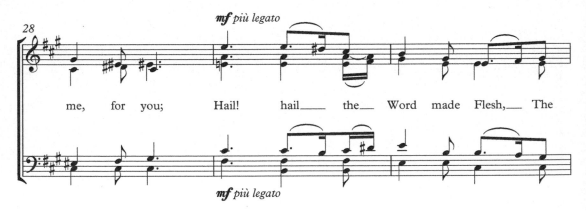

me, for you; Hail! hail___ the_ Word made Flesh,___ The

Babe,_ the Son__ of Ma - ry.___ So bring him in - cense,

Christ is born,___ The Babe,___ the Son___ of Ma - ry.

Raise, raise___ the___ song on high!___ The Vir - gin sings___ her

lul - la - by. Joy! joy!___ for___ Christ is born,___ The

Babe,___ the Son___ of Ma - - - ry.